GILBERT AND GARBO IN LOVE

A Romance in Poems

Gilbert and Garbo in Love

A Romance in Poems

Christopher Conlon

Capital Collection
THE WORD WORKS
WASHINGTON, DC

First Edition
First Printing
Gilbert and Garbo in Love: A Romance in Poems

The WORD WORKS
PO Box 42164
Washington, DC 20015
editor@wordworksdc.com

Book design, typography by Janice Olson
Cover design by Janice Olson

Production management: Marta Levcheva
Printed in Bulgaria

Library of Congress Number: 2002115065
International Standard Book Number: 0915380-54-4

Acknowledgments

Leatrice Gilbert Fountain's *Dark Star,* John Bainbridge's *Garbo,* and Anton Gronowicz's *Garbo: Her Story* were helpful to me for their biographical details. More generally, William K. Everson's *American Silent Film* and Scott Eyman's *The Speed of Sound* proved invaluable resources regarding early Hollywood.

I wish to thank Bernadette Geyer, Miles David Moore, and Hilary Tham for their sound editorial suggestions on this manuscript, as well as Janice Olson for her efforts on the design of the book and its cover. Finally, a grateful tip of the hat goes to Karren Alenier for inviting me in.

Contents

for Charlene,
who learned to love the silence

Small

At six he's big, he thinks, too big,
though normal for a child his age:
he sees others like him in the streets,
running, playing stickball and hopscotch.
But he's different. *Homes,* he ponders
as he watches them in their youthful
exuberance. *Those children have homes,*
and I don't have a home. Well,
he does have a home: Ida, his mother,
left him here; she often leaves him
for months with people she hardly knows.
So now he sits on the stoop of this hard
rat-laced brownstone in this hard
New York Irish neighborhood in
the hard summer of 1905. Sweating
in the sodden heat he looks out
across the faces, the horses, the motorcars
in the street, his knickers dirty, spotted
with oil and grime and drops of urine.
They have homes, he thinks again,
sounding the words in his mind
as if they were poetry. He remembers
the dark backstages of a dozen cities,
learning words from the dog-eared scripts
left on sawdusty floors, hearing Ida spit:
Every minute the little bastard gets bigger
is a minute I'm getting older. Big, big!
He stares at the children in their dresses
and hats, imagines willing himself
smaller, smaller still, so small that
the seamstress he's been left with
will stop yelling, stop telling him
she only has one room for God's sake,
what does he think visitors make of him
staring moony-eyed from the corner?
(One after another, four or five
a night sometimes, he's left alone

for hours and then the door clicks,
rattles, bursts open to her heavy
melodious trilling. *Here we are, love,*
she'll say, skeletal worm-pale woman
with bristles in her chin. He won't
be introduced. *Forget him, he ain't*
nothin'. The lights will go black
as the two of them drop onto the bed.
Sighs; creakings; a whispered *Jesus*
or *Yes* or *Shit* as he sits on blankets
in the corner, eyes shut tight,
fingers pressed into his ears, willing himself
away, projecting himself onto a stage
in a vast auditorium, grinning brilliantly
in flowing tuxedo and elegant tails,
applause engulfing him in warm waves,
his mother queenly in a vast frill-filled dress
and tiara, gazing adoringly up at him,
proud of him, so proud, loving him
at last, and taking him finally in her arms
and whispering, *My love, it's time to go home.*)
Yes, he thinks, staring at the grime-caked
street before him, at the ice vendors and milk
wagons, at the men strolling with their cigars
and the women with their laundry baskets, if only
he could make himself small, small enough,
smaller than a dog, than a gerbil,
smaller than a baseball, she would take him
back, drop him gently into her soft pocket
where the jostling warmth would hold him
safe always. And he can do it, he's sure,
if he tries, if he concentrates, if he puts
all his might into the attempt, and he shuts
his eyes, shuts out the shoutings and cabbage
smells of the street, tries to dissolve himself,
to shrink, expecting when he looks again
to find himself no bigger than a puppet,
or a toy soldier, or a picture in a nickelodeon:
tiny, perfect, worthy at last of home.

Beautiful

At eleven he's
beautiful: more so
than any boy should be.
Girls fifteen, sixteen
giggle toward him
in the darkness of
whatever city he's in.
Dark eyes, dark, eyes
that penetrate and seem
to see every secret you have,
to free you from every shame
you know. His stepfather
tells him that *Cecil* is no name
for a boy, insists on calling him
Jack, solid and manworthy,
and so he becomes
John Gilbert, Jack
to friends, and he has many.
Sometimes Ida takes him
on tours, allows him
to watch her rehearsing
with strangers in hollow
theaters like mausoleums.
Sometimes he steps out
a rear door into the dark, lights
a fugitive cigarette, listens
to the scratchings and rustlings
of city night. Sometimes
the giggles come very close,
sometimes there's breath
on his ear, sometimes a voice
says *Evening, dearie*, or
Ain't you the cute one.

He smells cabbage and sweet-
rancid melon as a hand
touches him, tugs
at his clothes. *For you*
it's free, love, it's always free
for someone beautiful as you.
He closes his eyes,
sees the world as a vast
empty stage of wind
and black stone, bereft
of life as it might have been
millions of years ago, in the first
nudgings of the universe.
He has a moment of light
then, and calm, as,
for a moment, he's
connected, one
with someone, anyone,
and the light bursts
upon his eyes and he is,
for an instant,
loved, and free.

Watching Ida Dress

Late light through the sheer curtain is like brass, dull
gold-yellow, and Jack feels it on his face as he watches
his mother, standing nude before the ornate hotel mirror,
dress. He loves her body: loves its sloping curves,
its dimples and unexpected downy hairs, the small soft
protuberance of her belly. Though he can't believe,
somehow, truly, that he was ever *in* her body, that they
could ever have been, once, one, for now he hardly exists
at all for her. He sits in the corner of the room, a room
like other rooms in a city whose name he's forgotten,
and knows that for her the room is empty. She coughs
once, twice, clears her throat, begins then with the combination,
pulling the shirt-and-panty over herself slowly, sighing
as she does it. A corset next, difficult to manage,
white and lacy yet somehow like armor, grunting as she
forces herself into the hard, tight material, fastening it
herself with metal clips in the front, contorting herself
before the mirror to grab at the laces in back, tightening them—
sometimes Jack is called upon to help with this, but not now—
and he watches as his mother's body is transformed,
turned uncannily slender even as she seems to have difficulty
breathing. She reaches to the dressing table, takes up
silk pads that attach to her hips and under her arms,
and this changes her body again, makes it curvaceous,
like a statue, Jack thinks, or a painting. Then her camisole,
her chemise, buttons, tapes, sounds of material pulled,
stretched, tied. She runs stockings up her legs, clips them
to garters clipped to the corset. At last she places her silk
petticoat around her in a circle, steps into it, lifts and ties it
around her waist. And so she is ready to put on her dress—
purple, flouncy, shabby-beautiful. To Jack
it makes her as lovely as Camille Clifford, Lillie Langtry,
any Gibson Girl, even as he sees that the sleeves are

frayed, the hem soiled. She wraps a black belt around herself,
nodding her head this way and that to the mirror. *Yes.*
She attaches gold earrings, a bright silver brooch,
three glittering necklaces, and slips her feet into little black
boots. From a chair behind her she takes up an enormous
ostrich-feathered hat, also purple, with a brim that angles
rakishly to one side, and sets it carefully atop her sweeping
Pompadour waves, adjusting it just so, in an operation
as delicate as surgery. *Yes, well, there were are*, she mutters
under her breath as she lifts white gloves from the table
and turns to leave the room. Before stepping out, Jack knows,
she'll gather her bag and parasol from the parlor,
keep them close to her like weapons. She'll go to rehearse
or meet men, her face pale, hysterically animated, and return
after dark, or not at all. But, sitting alone in the room
with the funny papers or Shakespeare, he loves to picture her
out there, in the glamorous world: there she is, head
thrown back in laughter, glass in her hand filled with fizzy
champagne, men in tuxedoes hanging on her every
witty word, and if she needs to cough she'll do it daintily,
so daintily that they'll hardly notice the sudden turning-away,
the raising of her hand to her mouth, or the handkerchief, speckled
now with bright black blood, that she folds quickly closed.

White Dark

The streets of Stockholm swirl
with snow, white on white so intense
that it seems to devour the dark itself,
make blinding noon at midnight.
Keta has separated from her
brother and sister, found her way
into an alley off Götegatan,
where she hears shouting voices—
she wants to go home, but everyone
in the neighborhood knows
about the Gustafssons, Anna and Karl,
Karl the butcher who comes home
smelling of blood and brain, Anna
who can match him blow for blow,
and how the children, Sven, Alva,
and little Greta whom they call Keta escape
out the back door into the white city dark.
Sometimes neighbors take them in,
coo over them, beautiful little Keta
especially, with her huge lovely eyes
and serious ways. Keta has heard
of a place called America, where the sun
always shines in a sky always blue,
where people ride in motorcars like chariots,
where the flickers, which she, six years old
in 1911, has never seen, project faces
forty feet high that live forever. But
all that is dreamtime. Now there's only
the alley, two drunks trying to fight
while half a dozen men cheer them on.
Blood drains from the smaller man's
nose. She watches, remembering blood
from her mother's nose, the doctor

in the middle of the night, his serious
words to Papi: *You really must not*
treat the mother of your children
this way, it's not right, you know.
Karl humble, regretful, as he would
always be, later, tears flying down
his face, grabbing at Keta, his favorite,
hugging her close. The snow
drops everywhere, on the fighting men,
the street, the ashcans, Keta's hair
and eyelashes. Snow, snow.
The smaller man falls and suddenly Keta
has pushed through the grownups, crying,
Stop! Stop! Can't you see he's beaten?
And, kneeling down, holding the man's
head, so like that of her father,
the same unfocused eyes and boozy stench,
she cradles it as she does her father's,
using the hem of her dress to wipe the blood
from his face, blood mixing with snow
in her dress as she whispers, again
and again, like a mantra she'll chant
all her life: *Beaten, beaten, beaten.*

Blekingegatan 32

This is the address that, though she can't know it
now, at ten or twelve, will always define home.
The view is of hard angles, cement blocks, another
apartment across the way gutted viciously by fire,
tracks of dirt and sand, bulldozers and dump trucks,
broken concrete, shale. The slums. Behind her:
shouts, curses, stumblings as her mother and father
wish death on each other. Someday, she knows,
she'll escape all this: become a writer, a singer,
an actress, and then she'll never think of this
foul gray pit again. She doesn't know that at thirty,
at sixty she'll dream of this place, this view,
she'll find herself alone and desolate staring out
at this vista of nothingness, hopeless, helpless,
voices she doesn't know ominous behind her,
malignant shadows swarming around her as she thinks,
I can't be home. I am home. Take me home.

Papi

Often he comes back, smelling of the creek-clear
brännvin he carries in a flask more carefully than a baby,
in a sentimental mood, his smile sliding sideways
across his face, his eyes soft and sagging in the kitchen
candlelight. He's Gösta Berling then, with Keta and the rest
as his cavaliers, sworn to do nothing sensible
or useful. Anna doesn't speak to him then, nor Sven or Alva;
only Keta, who heats onion-and-turnip soup for him, stirring it
with a cracked wooden spoon as Karl mumbles from his chair
God or *Bastards* or *More.* He'll drop his head into his hands
sometimes, telling her through wet sobs how she'll never know
the love he feels for her, for all of them. She'll sit next to him,
spoon-feed him the thin steaming soup, and if his head lolls suddenly,
his eyes roll back, she'll shout *Papi!* in a severe, schoolmarm tone.
Papi, wake up! Sometimes she slaps him, hard, and she can see
his eyes snap back into life then, glance at her in shock, then
grow easy, liquid, as a wet chuckle rises from his throat
and he swallows the soup she pushes at him, saying *Keta,*
darling Keta. Soup finished, he'll sleep for an hour or two
on the floor, until dawn sheets the windows. She'll make him
bitter coffee then, from old grounds, and watch him
stumble out the door to the butcher shop, twelve hours gone
sometimes, fourteen, in his life of blood, ligament, hacked bone.

Night and Day

Nights, his mother leaves
her hotel bed, her long gown
rustling as she creeps
stealthily into his.
She cradles his head
against her breast
as her tears touch
his cheek and she
whispers, *I'm sorry,*
Jackie, I'm sorry,
I love you, I swear
to God I do.

Days, she walks ahead
of him in the street, says
to people who come up
to her, recognize her:
That child? Mine?
Gracious! Go on, young
man, go peddle
your papers.
Go! Shoo!

Special

Watching his mother in sleep,
Jack thinks of how she's told him
he was born in the great summer storm
of 1899: the Logan River swelling,
exploding over the Wasatch Valley,
Utah's biggest flood in anyone's
memory. He likes the idea, likes
arriving with a bang, as if the earth
had somehow overflowed just
for him, burst its belly in cosmic joy
at his arrival. *Special*, he thinks,
it proves I'm special, and he holds
this thought in his mind as his mother's
eyelids flutter open and she demands
to know what the hell he's doing there.

Father

At night he dreams
of a father. A laborer,
ditch-digger, dirt thick
in his fingernails, skin
callused hard as horn,
missing teeth, hoarse
tobacco-heavy voice.
They live in a cabin
at the foot of a blue
mountain. He cooks
Jack dinner, they rough-
house, play cards, spit
manfully together, they spend
days wandering among yellow
wildflowers. His father
has never been to a theater,
has never even seen
a city. Night upon night
the two of them talk
quietly together in their cabin,
and fall asleep
under stars in summer
amidst long grass
stroked by wind.

Ways Out

Reading is Keta's earliest escape,
especially the stories of Selma Lagerlöf:
country life as it was lived long ago,
and written by a Swede! With a Nobel Prize!
She loves the feeling of sliding into another
world, one that opens into her skull,
casts spells, washes over her with wild
dream-visions. And the moving pictures:
those too, though they often don't have money
for admission. But she cuts the stars' photos
out of newspapers, magazines she finds
in ashcans: Wallace Reid, Raymond Griffith,
Betty Bronson, Lillian Gish, Mary Pickford,
the women as beautiful as the men, all of them
radiant soft-focused gods, or dreams
of gods, their faces forty feet high before her
enraptured upturned face. Each night she prays,
solemnly, seriously, silently, to lose herself
in those faces: beyond touching, beyond caressing,
to simply melt into them, become them,
make her final, bloodless, immortal escape.

Charity Ward

Twelve years old, thirteen, she takes her father
each week to the charity ward, blue water-streaked
walls, broken chairs, sits him down among
shadow-eyed prostitutes, rickety tuberculars.
He's made an effort this time, isn't drunk.
"Sober as a stone," he'd said proudly that morning,
to any in his family who would listen. Only Keta
did. He's convinced that what's wrong with him
won't be wrong with him if he's sober—after all,
it's the *brännvin* that's causing it, isn't that
what the doctor said? Keta remains with him
during the exam, even when she's asked
to leave: "No, she stays with me," he declares.
He strips off his shirt, exposes his pallid, lumpy
body, the doctor taps his back, listens to his heart.
"Karl," he says confidentially, leaning close to him
as if he wishes Keta not to hear, "you simply *must*
stop drinking. Don't you know that?" Her father
nods humbly, thanks the white-coated man, puts on
his shirt and tattered Homburg hat. "I stopped
already," he says to her on the way home, suddenly,
indignantly. "Doesn't he know that? Sober as a stone,
as a *stone*. Keta," he says finally, "you go on
home, yes? Papi has people he needs to see."
She obeys, always, always obeys, kisses him
on his stubbly cheek, says so long, Papi,
be well, moves up Götegaten toward the slums
and home, glancing back only once
to see him chatting with friends, tipping
his head back, flask to his lips: happy, she thinks,
as a boy, a boy finishing a race, or a test, or a boy
helping his girl up the steps to the abortionist's office.

Picnic by the Sea

Winter, and the sea is cold. The light is low,
the sky white, but Greta loves it here,
loves coming with her friends Mona and Mimi,
loves the feeling of icy air sheeting her skin,
loves the sensation of the entire ocean
smashing over face and breasts and thighs.
She loves to stretch out her arms toward Finland
and Russia and let the Baltic Sea knock her
over, ravish her until she's limp and senseless.
There's another sensation like this, one for which
she has no name: which she's found in the bathroom
at night, reaching up into herself. There's no one
she can ask, certainly not Mama or Alva, not Mona
or Mimi. She doesn't know what it is but knows it's secret.
Just for her. As now: arms wide, hair swept back, face
ecstatic: child-goddess, seraphic, serpentine, perfect.

Ida's Death

On the day his mother dies
the sun doesn't vanish from the sky,
no one weeps in the streets,
flags aren't dropped to half-mast,
the papers print no special editions.

On the day his mother dies
libraries open and close as scheduled,
shopkeepers bag groceries and make change,
old men complain about weather,
women buy hats.

On the day his mother dies
teachers give him looks of sympathy,
trolley car conductors let him ride for free,
his father stays gone; and he begins
to grasp, dimly, some of the workings of the world.

Karl's Death

For months he's nearly dead, skeletal, never not
in bed, and Greta, thirteen, feeds him by hand,
changes his shit-stained sheets, empties the milk bottle
filled with his pale yellow flow. Friends visit
at first, sneak him *brännvin*, but they flicker out
and soon it's only the two of them, all others
banned from the room. Candles, shadows.
Cold. Death-stench. Day and night, slow hell–
but she would be nowhere else. When it happens
his hand is in hers and she feels a spirit ascend, not his
but hers, suddenly, shockingly free, rising sunlit
into the world, the moment she sheds what's left
of herself, begins, at last, to be born, to grieve.

Thirteen

In San Francisco he scrubs barroom floors
and rinses out spittoons, sleeps in the back
on old horse blankets and straw, eats
bar food—eggs, boiled cabbage, blood
sausage. He's thirteen and it's not bad,
not really. He likes the night streets,
fogbanked and frigid, outlines of passersby
vague, ethereal, like something from his
dreams. Sometimes he'll see a woman
with a big feathered hat and flouncy dress,
red or blue or purple, float toward him
in the dark, and she's Ida, his mother,
and then isn't. But she's so many
of them—a dozen times he moves
toward an eye, a cheekbone, a shoulder,
certain for a moment it's her. Sometimes
she'll smile at him, nod her head, lead him
into the nearest alley, help him to shoot off
onto a grease-streaked wall. She'll want
a nickel, a dime, whatever he'll give, and then
he's back in the streets again, damp, cold,
three a.m., four—searching for solace,
comfort, hunting always for morning.

Soaplather Girl

White-smocked, she mixes hot lather and sinks
gray bristle-brushes into it, turns, smears the smiling
men's faces with it expertly, quick circular strokes.
She dreams of being an actress, knows this
to be a type of acting: to allow her hand to graze
the stubble faces, a touch so gentle they don't know,
for a moment, if it even happened. Or a soft
glance sliding quickly across them, or leaning
her face just slightly closer to them than she needs to.
She sees them respond, the young men and the
old ones, the harried bankers and sallow
street sweepers, sees their fast grins and hopesick
eyes. She feels their heat rising to her in waves,
not from the lather but from other, secret sources.
She smiles, doesn't speak, promises nothing.
Fourteen, she wouldn't know what to promise
even if she would. She accepts their coins
gratefully, certain that someday she'll understand
why they give them, and why they give her the look they do
as they leave: part joy, part pain, part cold contempt.

Extry

He's unloading crates on a dock
one day when he hears two men
talking about the pictures. *Top dollar*
in them flickers, one says, telling
of a friend good with horses
who headed down that way and
makes twenty-five a week now, easy,
riding, roping, shooting and being shot.
They call 'im an extry, he says,
old salt-sailor, *an' he's got*
all the women he wants, too.
Hell, Jack can ride, a little. He sees
the moving-picture town in his mind
(Holly-something? wood?), all palm
trees and desert-sharp skies, freedom,
lungfuls of air like hot fists in his chest–
knows then he'll try it, hop a freight
south, introduce himself around, tell them
he'll ride for twenty-five a week, hell yes.
A year or two of it, maybe, save some
cash, then light out again: Mexico,
South America, be a bandit,
a smuggler, a rogue, a crook, whatever
he wants, whatever in the world.
It's his, it belongs to him, all of it–
he'll be anyone, everyone he wants to be!

Hats

She finds in the camera lens something alluring,
yet a challenge too, and plays to it, unafraid,
even joyful, removing one silly felt or straw number
after another, plopping the next onto her head,
pouting, grinning, jutting her jaw and glancing shyly
away. All theater games, nothing but playacting:
the camera lens can be her lover, if only
for the instant it takes to flash the photo. Yes:
love, she thinks, loving, as it may be someday
with some man. She could do this forever,
maybe will, stand starkly in the bright bursts,
she could do it drunk, could do it naked.
She's the center of the universe and knows it.
Unmatched ecstasy! Only later will she learn
never to look at what the lens records
of her: never behold the bulging eyes, the
harsh-angled face, little Keta Gustafsson
peering out from the page, timorous, stupid,
staggering down Stockholm slum alleys
apologizing, worth only a curse, a slap,
a good hard blow.

Camera

Sixteen and he's the damn fool
grinning into the camera as he
gallops past on a white steed,
one of thirty-eight Yankees.
Later he'll slip into a Rebel's uniform,
charge back the other way;
spliced, the thirty-eight of them
will ambush themselves. Such
madness! Such fun! He loves
to sneak into the rushes, gaze up
at the glowing images as they
careen forward and back, are
slowed, stopped, started again,
and he glimpses himself now and then,
bright white face in a white sea.
But this day he sinks into his seat,
lowers his cap over his eyes as
the producer waves his cigar
at the screen and screams,
Who's that idiot looking
into the camera? They stop
the picture, slowly reverse it,
thread one frame at a time through
the projector until, yes, there he is,
Jack Gilbert, caroming by in a blur
but not *quite* a blur, his head turned
straight to the camera, grin gleaming
out to the world. *Fire that son*
of a bitch! the producer bellows,
gesticulating wildly, and an underling
assures him it will be done, sir. But
the next day Jack reports to work
as usual, attacks himself as usual,
whoops and roars with the rest
and, every now and then,
steals a secret rascal's glance
straight into the camera's eye.

Screen Test

The glare in her eyes is hotter than sun, and
brighter. She wonders if the makeup is melting
from her face. Somewhere, out there in the dark,
she can just make out The Director: his wild,
fervid eyes, his scowl of disgust as he shouts
at her: *Act! For God's sake, act!* She acts.
His voice booms, reverberating through the
sepulchral studio: *Turn left! Turn right! Look*
joyful! Look angry! Act, act, you bitch, act!
The camera clatters like a train rushing
at her future. The Director's voice commands her
to grieve: *Your lover is dead!* She looks up:
stares straight into a blinding light, her head
seems to burst, white on white, she feels tears
drop down her face, hears a cry of anguish
from far away and abruptly collapses onto the floor.

Later, in a room of cool darkness, The Director will hold
a damp cloth to her forehead, coo gently to her.
You show promise, Greta, he will say.
But to learn the art of acting you will need
years of my discipline. Are you ready, my child?

Hollywood's End

Dusk. Behind him, in another world, the shore, salt-scented
air, sellers of hot dogs and ices, the vast sea. But here, miles
and miles inland (past the studio lots with their Civil War
battlefields, their Babylonian temples, their little French
villages and English manor houses, all so perfectly real
unless he looks behind the facades, sees the plywood
and paint and gray nails), Jack finds the end of the road:
paved street that becomes dirt track, then nothing at all,
dirt dissolving into dirt-desert before him. It's 1915, he
makes fifteen dollars a week as an extra, dreams one day
of having a scene of his own, just one scene. He could walk,
he thinks, out into this desert, live another life: prospector,
miner for gold, the land so starkly beautiful, so austere,
scrub brush and cactus and mountains brown and hard
as sunburned fists, the sky so impossibly large, hawks
cruising fearlessly on the horizon. It's then he hears a sizzling,
like steaks on a grill, looks down: a glistening snake,
Mojave rattler, partly coiled, tongue flashing, tangoes
toward him. He stands speechless, only a little afraid,
between one life and another, chewing his lip, deciding
which way to move, which way more real, which safe.

The Director

Eyes the color of ocean, hundreds of miles distant
from sunlight, one encircled in a silver-rimmed monocle.
Eyes cutting, as if they could parse light itself,
air, find their way to her secret places, the ones
that murmur to her in the night of how she killed
her father, didn't she—happy at his death,
free? Selfish, spiteful, useless bitch!
Eyes that travel inside her in dreams, light beams
crisscrossing through her heart, brain, illuminating,
exposing every lie she's lived. Once he demands
she strip before him for costume tests, just the two
of them in his ornate Stockholm hotel suite,
and she does, without question: eyes watching her
as he tosses one costume after another
into her arms. *Try this one. God, no. This one.*
She does it mechanically, thoughtlessly,
watching his eyes watch her with clothes
and without, naked beyond reckoning, naked
as no one could ever be naked: sinking
through the dark of his eyes, seduced, ravished,
raped by his eyes, ripped apart from within
by his eyes, consumed, transformed by his eyes,
she's his, only, only his, she'll live forever in his eyes.

Jack Famous

Slow growth: moving up Motor Avenue or down
Sunset Boulevard on a sun-drenched Saturday in 1919,
1920, he might notice two ladies across the street,
conferring behind their hands: *Who is that man?*
Isn't he in the moving pictures? Perhaps a nod then,
a little wave from their tight white gloves, uncertain quite
who he is, but sure that he must be someone.
But then—ah—1925, Von Stroheim, *The Merry Widow:*
no one ever again would not know his name.
Oh my Lord it's John Gilbert they chitter breathlessly,
giggling like girls, twisting their hips, curling their hair
in their fingers, stumbling as they reach their hands
to his, stammering foolishly, dropping their autograph
books, forgetting their names. He feels then like a patient
Papa with his clumsy daughters, comforting them,
encouraging them, bestowing perhaps a smile or,
for the older and more matronly ones, a chaste
and gentlemanly kiss on their brown-spotted hands.
He loves them! Loves them all! Deliberately walks
sometimes when he might drive or be driven, just
for this: the look, the gasp, the fluttering feet—evidence,
proof positive that the dashing figure on the screen
of light is himself, his deepest, best self, John Gilbert,
utterly real, their dream made flesh, bone, thundering heart.

America

A few films and she's famous, a little,
in her little country, she and The Director.
But this is nothing, he scoffs: Peasants!
Farmers! Garbage-eaters! America,
America it must be, and soon is:
goodbyes at the dock, Greta weeping
into her mother's bosom, The Director
checking his watch again and again.
They sleep chastely, in different cabins,
despite her pleas that they stay together,
not for any indecent reasons, God no,
but just for company, companionship.
Stupid little schoolgirl, he mutters,
slamming his door in her face.

She'll wander the deck for hours
at night, breathing the sea-spray,
imagining dropping away into space,
splashing down through the depths
to live with sharks and squid.
When she sleeps at last
the ship will be a mausoleum,
her dark cabin a coffin, and in the morning
he'll kill her, obliterate her with
a few words and sheets of paper:
You must forget Keta Gustafsson.
Think of her as dead. And so she becomes
someone new, newly named. Alone, she'll try
the syllables on her tongue: *Gar. Bo. Gar-bo.*
Greta Garbo, she thinks, heading
to America: to paradise, to greatness,
part bright star, part shambling corpse.

Questions

He's married for a while,
but like so much in his life now,
she never seems, somehow,
quite real: her voice
beside him at night, his in-laws
at the dinner table:
Who are these people?
And the cinema faces he greets
at the studio, the millionaires
like Mayer who call him *Jack,*
the gate guards who doff their hats
reverently, say, *Good morning,*
Mr. Gilbert; are they real?
Are they actors, playing parts?
When he turns his back,
do they vanish?
Why do they honor him?
Who is he?
What, for God's sake, is his life?

The Director: Discovery

She'll dream of his eyes for the rest of her life.
Blue-black, depthless: eyes she could fall into,
become lost in, maybe did. She'd heard strange sounds,
slappings and bangings, in the next room, and, wakened,
crossed in her nightgown to the connecting door.
Her feet were warm in the plush carpet and the lights
of New York glistened outside in the rain. Why, why
wasn't the door locked? Why, why did she open it?
But it wasn't, and she did, and his eyes—the chandelier
blazed—cut through her, their expression wild, accusing,
as she stammered the start of an apology, backed
quickly out, stumbled, felt pain sting her toe, slammed
the door again, tried to blank out the twisted limbs,
the boy's body, pale, skinny, no more than twelve
or thirteen. *Cut!* she wants to cry, as he does. Cut,
do the scene over, this time, God, this time without the boy.
A week before he'd taken her virginity, held it
in his hand, kissed it, told her what a treasure
it was, how love would entrance them
always. The room dim, and the smell of roses. His eyes:
the last she'd see, she thought: the last she'd ever need to see.

Death of Valentino

Ah, mad procession! Ghastly parade! Dozens of black
Rolls-Royces, thousands of weeping women lining
the streets, strewing flowers. Morbid, hysterical,
garish scene, a thing out of some crazed melodrama
by that madman O'Neill. Jack wonders what it feels like
to be Valentino now: Heaven? Limbo? Hard black
cancellation, nothingness? But even as he thinks it
he feels the eyes of the world's women moving
toward him, over him, engulfing him, millions of eyes,
with them breaths and gasps, voices, visions—yes,
this is it—his titanic form of shadow and light sliding
into the liquid daydreams of the high school girls
and the hard pornographic fantasies of the housewives.
He wishes he could be less happy than he is right now.
Good God, it's indecent! He slicks back his hair
in the mirror, adjusts his somber black tie, prepares himself
to praise and bury the King, but can't stifle an impudent
child's grin of absolute euphoria, sweet torchlight
passing brightly into his heart: *The King is dead...Long,*
yes, long, O, long, long, long live the King!

The Director: Career

He drinks, he screams,
he's fired. The old story.
She watches him watching her
no longer needing him.
Lurching wraith, he lurks
in corners. She tries with him
for a while, then stops
trying. The old story. Down,
he flares out and down,
gets fat, grows ludicrous,
magician without magic,
flat-footed, deflated,
collapsing alone in the dawn
of freedom's land.
She pictures him pissed-on,
mutilated, skin shredded
by wolves, eyes crow-gutted.
The old story. She pictures herself
cradling his broken body,
whispering to him, chantlike,
that he's beaten, beaten, beaten.

The House on Tower Road

It's a tower itself, a palace, ludicrously
ornate, something a prince from the Far East
might build for himself, his wives, his children,
his slaves, his harem. Good God! Marble
everywhere! Ceilings so high it's as if
they're not there at all! Arched doorways,
Spanish-style, bright frescoes in imitation
of some other place and century, he
doesn't know which, cavernous sunken
bathtubs with sunbright brass fittings,
and, just outside, the pool, and acres
of aroma-rich orange trees, a mirror-black
Rolls in the driveway, and Pola Negri
his neighbor, Fatty Arbuckle just up the street:
it's his life, he thinks, in this spring of 1925,
his star's life, money gushing from everywhere
at once, and this is the life he was born
to lead, must lead, *shall* lead, without a chance
in heaven it could ever be taken away by anyone.

The Director: Funeral

His eyes are shut. She's free.
His hands are still. She's free.
His voice is stopped. She's free.

Her life is hers. She's free.
Her choices are hers. She's free.
Her lovers are hers. She's free.

She turns away. She's free.
She leaves the church. She's free.
She hails a cab. She's free.

She weeps, she screams. She's free.
She wants him, wants him. She's free.
She's lost, she's shit. She's free.

Oh!

When Greta meets Jack for the first time
he's *Mr. Gilbert* and her ass is sticking up
in the air. She's trying to tie her shoe
and he's walked up behind her, just like that,
said, *Miss Garbo?* and it's her ass, her goddamn
ass he's talking to. She nearly falls
when she turns and sees him: he seems
supernatural in his beauty, his immensity.
Oh! she gasps, breathless, pushing the hair
back from her face, smoothing her skirt.
He grins, beneficent. *We're to be co-stars,*
I believe, he intones smoothly, elegantly,
his voice surprisingly light but cultured,
articulate, suave. *I'm delighted,* he goes on
(unfazed, amused at her giddy fear),
to make your acquaintance at last.
In response she loses her footing, stumbles
backward, covers her mouth, cries, *Oh!*

Later Jack will smile, confiding to a friend:
Lovely girl, really. But she'd best hope
they never develop the talking pictures!

The Studio Lot at Midnight

Arms interlocked, the silence between them warm
and content, there's no other place they can even imagine
wanting to be. How real, this: Dodge City or Amazon jungle,
Paris or darkest Africa, all empty, uninhabited worlds
entirely theirs to share, without agents or makeup men
or producers or fans jostling them on the street cadging
an autograph, a touch, a buck from *Gilbert* or *Garbo* who seem,
sometimes, to themselves, less real than dreams; roles,
put-ons that others animate, keep alive, love, try
to tear down. Here, now, nothing is wanted of them
by anyone. They live, for a few minutes at least, only
for each other. Their shoes scuff softly through the dark
interstices, worlds between worlds, neither of them in any
hurry to reach Athens or Rome, happy to pause in Bethlehem
or even Hollywood, to share a cigarette, a word, a slow kiss,
their only abiding company the patient and radiant stars.

Two People

Today they're the two most
beautiful people on earth, ordained so
by a poll in a fan magazine,
and they are sunk together in bear skin
before a flickering fire, rain
thrumming outside,
and they are the only two
people on earth, the only limbs on earth,
the only breaths and tongues on earth,
while millions of rain eyes gaze in at them
through the windows, wistful and envious.

Yes

She'll know someday that this
was joy, but now, in this moment,
she knows only the day:
windows open to the lawn,
bright shadowless noon,
she drinks wine, strokes him
so that he comes four times, five,
in minutes, all effortlessly, and she
spreads it over her skin, her belly
and breasts, her lips, dabs it
behind her earlobes, unable not
to laugh, to shout and cry out,
wanting only more of him, all of him,
over her, around her, inside her,
him, him only, him always, the bed
their altar and cradle, motionless
in time, in space, everything achieved,
life transcended, death toppled,
the two of them one poetry, one verse,
one word forever. *Yes.*

Interlude

i.

The odor of orange blossoms
fills the sun-filled air. Jack watches
the curtain waft in the warm California
breeze, feels her damp hair on his arm,
listens to her slow sleeping breath.
A petal flutters in, dances for a moment,
drifts silently down to her cheek:
white pale-fading into white.

ii.

She stirs, pleasantly uncertain
who she is or where. The ceiling
is so high, the huge arches like something
in a museum or fairy tale. She pushes
her face into the crook of his arm,
remembers, sighs, feels herself melting
back into sleep, love, dream.

iii.

Three o'clock in the afternoon. The faraway
chopping sound of lawnmowers, the smell
of grass mixed with orange blossoms and,
somewhere, eucalyptus. Their faces
almost touching, their bodies entwined,
the sheets like sod for their quiet rooting
and growth.

iv.

He watches the light shift from lemon
to peach, from peach to rose. Watches
her skin absorb each tone, changing

her eyelids and lips, fingers and breasts,
minute-to-minute a new woman, unexpected,
never not beautiful.

v.

She hears a church bell sound six,
feels his body pressed beside her,
wants nothing now but his deep warmth
to engulf her, overwhelm her, set her free.

vi.

Neither knows when they begin
to make love again. Their pulse
flows, their blood rushes, their body
one body, opening, surging, gushing,
sinking back stunned and satiated.
Dozens of orange petals float onto them
as they embrace, and they will sleep
under them now, forever:
their own private garden, themselves.

Mayer Sees It All

Later, after the pheasant and sweet grapes,
the California cantaloupe and strawberries and wine,
the two of them watch as Mayer kicks his feet up
in his leather-lined study, sighs contentedly,
shares brandy and cigars with them (Greta—why
not?—has one too), and, puffing, watching them
closely, reveals his vision. "One of the boys,"
he says, referring to his flunkies and yes-men,
"gave me this book." He tosses it onto the table.
"Sure, it's a 'classic,'" he says, the word clearly
sour in his mouth, "but it'll be big, I promise
you. *Big*. For the two of you. I didn't read it,
but he told me about it. *Big* passion. *Big*
feeling. A *weeper*." He scowls at the book.
"We'll have to change the title, naturally.
Anna is all right, but *Karenina*—what's that,
a new goddamned brand of soap? 'Caress
Your Skin With Karenina'? Ha!" They watch
as Mayer's eyes begin to glow mysteriously,
enlarge, as his face is suffused suddenly with
a nearly religious awe. His voice grows very
quiet. "I give you this," he says to his two
biggest stars. "I give you *Love*." He grins then,
lets out a whoop. Jack and Greta smile, say
not a word. "Good Lord," he goes on, "it's brilliant!
Brilliant! Every marquee in America! Talk about
exploitation! Talk about *showmanship!*"
He forms a rectangle with his hands and intones,
for the first time in the history of the world,
his magic words: "Gilbert and Garbo...in *Love*."

Gilbert and Garbo in Love

1.

Jack can't get enough of the daily rushes,
watching the unedited footage glow, become
luminous, alive, gazing at the two of them, two
poor kids and some phony, makeshift sets
become a world. He's never not aware
of the camera, his angle and lighting,
his expression. He's in the scene
but above it too, beyond it, as, he thinks,
geniuses and madmen are: he watches himself,
a child's glee warming him as he sees the scene
is his. He murmurs Count Vronsky's love-words
to her, grins a little. He arches his eyebrow,
knowing it'll give the farmers' wives a thrill.
Step right up! he wants to shout,
P.T. Barnum-style. *Get your comedy here, folks,*
get your pathos–get it all right here in the world's
biggest star–the amazing Jack Gilbert!

2.

Greta never attends the rushes.
Can't bear them, can't stand herself
on the screen: Stockholm again, Keta Gustafsson,
little fat-face. *Burn it,* she thinks, *burn it all,*
let no one see my shame. She can't act
and knows it. Hasn't the technique
of a Gish, the range or depth of a Norma Talmadge.
All she can do is be in a scene, focus everything
to the pinpoint moment of it, be there
and nowhere else, lost in her lover's eyes, the eyes
she would follow anywhere. Who's Anna?
Who's Vronsky? She doesn't know. It doesn't
matter. It's *her,* she and Jack alone together,
she's lost, lost in his eyes, aching at his touch.
It's not technique, she knows, not acting:
merely being. Somehow, it will have to do.

Living in Sin

He watches her from their bed, her body glowing
translucently in the Southern California morning,
light spilling through the curtains that nod in the sea
breeze. He's where he wants to be and will never want
to be anywhere different. She wears his pajama bottoms,
nothing else, brushes her teeth with wild energy,
her back undulating as she does it. He hears her spit
and gargle. He'll never tire of these sounds, these
sights: her sleep-puffed eyes, her pillow-matted hair.
They'll grow old together—sudden vision!—in this house,
living together, loving together, raising children together,
they'll greet the Jules Verne years of 1940 and 1960
together, perhaps try the theater together as they age...
She turns to him, grins, scampers girlishly at him,
flings herself on their bed, laughs, clamps her arms
around his neck, presses her breasts hotly
against his chest, kisses him, coos love-words to him;
no, thank God, there's nothing for either of them but this,
this grandness and glory, this early summer of 1927:
Gilbert and Garbo, sun-warmed, satisfied, untouchable, supreme.

Movies

They lie naked together under a wool blanket
on a high breezy hill, images of themselves
blanketing the sky above them, ten thousand feet
high, so lustrous they blot out all but a few determined
stars peeping through. It frightens them, this
largeness, this luminosity, they fear that perhaps
the images are more real than they are: bigger,
brighter, angelic, everlasting, so much closer
than their own souls might ever come to heaven.

Cold

Sometimes she feels the Stockholm snows
have never left her: that they lie still
pocketed in her brain, her tendons, her spine.
Coldness in California's fairyland sun. She needs
sweaters when everyone else is in shirtsleeves,
wears slacks rather than breezy dresses.
He cannot, ever, hold her close enough, keep her
warm enough, safe enough. He folds himself
around her, into her, comforts her the entire
night through: not enough. Something holds
the snow within her too deeply, unreachably.
Greta, he whispers, *Greta Gustafsson*
from Stockholm, my little Keta. She stiffens.
Don't, she whispers in return, *don't call me*
that, I'm not Keta, there is no more Keta,
Keta is dead. She says it again, repeats it over
and over, as if by saying it she can make it true,
while snow calcifies like tumor around her heart.

Dreams

1. Jack

He's curled fetally
in his mother's palm,
sleeping gently,
as her fingers close slowly
around him—his eyes snapping open
a moment too late.

2. Greta

She's floating in warm white
sun, a girl six or seven
in a daisy-yellow dress,
but she's herself too, grown woman
reaching up from darkness toward
a bright pretty child, knowing
she's fallen too far to ever
be worthy of her salvation.

Greta and Garbo

But when she's alone, in her dressing room, she knows,
or in her bath: that it's all a kind of confidence game. She knows
she's not that lambent and graceful spirit they see on screen, knows
the ones who rush to her gasping *Garbo* are dupes, knows
they're like country yokels tricked by a cardsharp. She knows
how she disappoints in person: *That* bony woman? she knows
they ask themselves, *that's* Garbo? She's no magician, she knows,
in life, only when projected glowingly forty feet high. She knows
what she does isn't acting, not really, but modeling. She knows
the difference. She stands and is photographed and knows
that when the photos flash through a clattering projector, knows
when her image is thrown up blindly into blackness, knows
that it's then the one they call *Garbo* is made. She knows
too that they can have her, have Garbo all for themselves, knows
that she just wants, for God's sake, to be let alone. She knows
this. *Garbo,* the mad wraith who pursues her: she knows
she can never truly escape her, never really be free, knows
that wigs, sunglasses, armed guards are her future: knows
she can only hide as *Garbo* runs riot in the world, all-knowing.

Science Fiction

Home early from a film—*Metropolis,* garish future-fantasy—
Greta drops immediately into bed, her mind overrun
with waves of geometric light: antiseptic cityscapes,
strange contraptions of a twenty-first century she'll never see.
Toward morning, sunrise touching her eyelids, she dreams
herself as a robot: coming to consciousness in a dark
laboratory, Jack there running a magic wand up
and down her gold-metal body, and she knows he's created
her, that he's mentor, father, God. She loves her metal shell,
loves the hard burnished sheen of it, its near-indestructibility;
but when he begins to kiss her, caress and make love to her,
she sprouts flesh—soft white moss that covers
her over. By the time they finish she's beautiful—
she knows she's beautiful—crystal-blue eyes, smooth
brunette hair: and she loves him for this, will always
love him for this: for making her human, whole;
they'll drink chamomile tea together every evening
for a thousand years. But in moments alone she'll pull back
the skin he's given her like webbing, touch again her smooth
metal core, remember that this is, somehow, her real self:
inviolate, secret, perfectly safe, never truly touchable.

Getaway

They drive up to Santa Barbara on a whim
one December Saturday, Highway One
keeping the sea near them like a heartbeat.
Jack wears a floppy hat and overcoat,
Greta sunglasses and a rancher's fur-lined
jacket: no one knows them. Off-season, anyway,
the beach to themselves, wandering for hours,
picking shells from the surf, stopping
for fried fish and french fries—greasy, delicious.
They make their way to the end of the long
pier, the hazy horizon endless distances
away, and toss bread from a paper bag
to swooping Pacific gulls. With astonishment
he realizes she's crying; that he is, too.
They look away from each other, gaze
at gulls, throw bread until the sack is empty
and the birds lose interest, glide off.
Neither of them speaks of it: not on the walk
to the car or the drive south to Los Angeles
again, back to their names, their lives. Unspoken,
it sinks to shadows; strange, indigestible,
drowning unclaimed in the black winter sea.

Unwritten Words

He would write:
I wish I could tell you what I feel my love

She would write:
I wish you could tell me what I feel my love

He would write:
Words are too small for us my love

She would write:
Words are all for us my love

He would write:
Be with me forever my love

She would write:
Be with me now my love

He would write:
How can I live without you my love

She would write:
How can I live my love

He would write:
Save me my love

She would write:
Save me my love

He would write:
Save me my love

She would write:
Save me my love

Evidence

Her body is dazzled by his, electrified,
heart smashing in her chest, throat constricted,
fingertips astonished, nerves berserk, and
she cries uncontrollably with him, tears
of love, of childish glee, of honest, humble gratitude:
nothing, nothing in the world for her, ever, but this!

And yet after the end, separate again, touching only
shoulders or hands or interlocking feet, she's
overcome with remorse, dark sadness emanating
from a place deeper than she can name,
spreading sickly throughout her, overwhelming
her: it's beyond words, beyond weeping, nothing she
or anyone can know. *Empty. Dead.* She doesn't
deserve this. *Desolate. Black.* She doesn't
deserve this. *Suffocating. Nothing.* She doesn't
deserve this. If only he'd do something so she'd know,
truly, finally, consummation; so she'd know, truly,
finally, how much he loves her: kick her, maybe,
slap her, punch her in the face, piss on her,
make her eat her own shit. Yes.

The Wedding

She leaves him waiting at the altar,
leaves him waiting, just leaves him,
puts on dark sunglasses and catches
a matinee uptown. It's little more
than an equation in her mind. He's
there, of course, and three hundred
guests, thousands upon thousands
of dollars of catering paid for by MGM.
One bride, mysteriously vanished;
they'll comb the city for her, search
hospitals, hope to God she's dead
or at least delirious. She goes
to the library, finds a copy of
Gösta Berling in English,
reads down the afternoon.

He'll find her in their bed
hours later, she'll feel the tension
in his touch. They'll say
nothing of it, know only that a
threshold has been reached, looked over,
turned away from. Now, at last,
they can truly love, love forever,
now that they both know it's over.

At the Premiere of The Jazz Singer

He holds a frozen grin throughout it—dashing, incandescent,
inimitable. Afterward, resplendent in tie-and-tails, he poses
with this-or-that star, newsreel cameras clacking, photo flash
bulbs popping. He feels himself starting to sweat, tries to excuse
himself, but the men with press passes in their hats insist
on their questions: *What's the potential for these so-called
'talkers,' Jack?* He grins, grins, nods affably, admits they're
Charming, a charming novelty but that *They have no
future, nothing can replace the elegance of the pantomime.*
The bulbs burst in his face like suns, his head throbs, the voices
jabber at him, he twists away, stumbles into the nearest
limousine, crying *For God's sake, go!* at the faceless driver
before him, desperate suddenly to outrush the future
which even now bears down on him like a blast of trumpets.

Are You Afraid?

He dreams   that night   of a golden   city hurled
into wet rancid   darkness   the beautiful naked
children of the city   (they are all children   in the city)
jumping desperately   backward into boiling   churning seas
        miles down miles   flailing waving the end
                of the world
        screaming hordes splintering   the gates
but the children all   the children dropping   in silence
in terror in silence   in tears in silence   dropping
                in silence

White Voice

Everyone knows there's trouble. Sound men
glance fretfully at each other; directors ask
for dozens of retakes. Voice coaches teach him
to breathe from his diaphragm, technicians monkey
with the equipment: useless. Something happens
when his voice is electrified, channeled invisibly
through Vitaphone wires and relays, carved
into grooves on hard shellac discs to be replayed
with his moving lips: the highs grow adenoidal,
nasal, the lows disintegrate and disappear.
White voice, he hears someone say. *Gilbert's got*
a white voice. All top, no bottom. Impossible.
The laughter in the theaters drowns the dialogue,
drowns him. *Falsetto* and *squeaky* and *girlish*
attach themselves to his name like tin cans
on a dog's tail. *Has-been. Failure. Joke.*
Producers he's known for years stop returning
his calls. Others who struggle with sound
get this consolation: *Not as bad as Gilbert.*
Like a factory worker when the only plant in town
slams its gates shut, he's suddenly jobless; nothing
but time when the long mornings rise. He wanders
streets, knocks on doors that don't open. He's
tainted, he knows, smells of mortality. He stops
in bars, in liquor stores, reads *Variety,* sits on benches.
The California sun pours over him in mute, glorious witness.

The Young Lions, Roaring

How they talk! All those words!
Their names new, unfamiliar, their faces
different, somehow harder, more real,
yes, but in a smaller way. Robinson,
Cagney, Muni, even the young man
Gary Cooper (whom Jack remembers
as an extra: nice boy, eye for the ladies,
reminded him of himself then). And damned
Gable, stealing his part in *Red Dust,*
and Colman, his image "like John Gilbert
in the old days," but with that rich velvet
baritone, absolute music. Jack tries,
tries, but: words! so many of them, rapid-fire
Gatling-gun deliveries, so many
to remember, to inflect just so like a stage
actor, and he isn't, damn it all, he isn't
a stage actor, he's a pantomimist, a figure
of gestures and expressions in a world
of cacophonous Vitaphone. He sees them,
all of them, marching past him, talking
and singing their way into the bold future
of the unimaginable 1930s, a parade of them:
he opens his mouth to protest, to cry out,
but their voices overwhelm him, and he's silenced.

Garbo Talks!

Silents, she thinks, were made in sound: workmen sawing, directors
shouting, all while she lost herself in the scene and the camera
rolled—pleasant beehive. But talkies are made in silence: everyone
everywhere absolutely still, mute, while the microphone lurks just
out of sight, unobtrusive as a hand grenade. She's watched others:
the stammering, the clearing of throats, the Oh God I'm sorrys;
Clara Bow, terrified, exasperated, actually grabbing the thing
and pummeling it with her fists. And, ah, she's watched Jack,
smooth, professional, but the voice—no. It's over for him, she knows,
he's doomed. But she won't be, can't be. Never mind her nerves,
never mind that English isn't even her language, damn the mike,
damn the sepulchral silence all around her, all she sees now
are the slum alleys of Stockholm again, cold, hunger, useless
Keta-mouth-to-feed, smells the blood on her father's apron, feels
its stickiness on her fingers, no, better to be dead than that, *no.*
She sits at the barroom table. The set is silent, the cast, the crew.
She senses an enormous suspended inhalation of breath as she
opens
her mouth, says simply, clearly: *Gimme a visky,*
ginger ale on the side. And don't be stingy, baby.
Silence then, so much silence. The director nods, slowly,
then quickly. The soundman in the booth
nods. Smiles. Thumbs-up. And when they watch the rushes later,
without her, they'll applaud, all of them, crew, front office, studio,
city, country: *Garbo talks, and the world loves her for it!*

Alone in her dressing room, the news brought to her by a friendly
errand-boy, she'll thank God, Christ, anyone, as she shakes wildly,
tears zigzagging down her face: deportation, starvation,
the black future like a runaway train rushing at her, lights flashing,
horn screaming; but ducked at the last instant, miraculously
rescued.

Pity

She's a diaphanous ghost now, inhabiting the guest bedroom
down the hall.
They see each other rarely, even more rarely speak. He watches
her from the far
end of the long mahogany corridor in her gauzy white robes
and nightgowns, bare feet
making no sound he hears. Yet she's so close. Once—he can't
help himself—
he calls softly to her, as if they were children up late, afraid of
being caught: *Greta?*
She turns, distant figure in darkness, surprised, unsure perhaps
what she's heard,
if anything. Finally she creeps partway up the hall, peers
uncertainly at him, whispers
What is it? But he can't explain. She senses it, or something,
and comes close
to him, not impatient, not unkind. *What is it, Jack, what?* He
touches her, she
draws back, but not away, and he's nearly weeping. Somehow
they're on the bed
then, his bed, their bed, outside time again, before failure,
catastrophe, and it's
as it was, yes, just as it was until he looks closely at her face in
the darkness
and sees it, sees the pity unmistakably suffusing her eyes.
Appalled, he pulls away,
wanting to stand, to order her with dignity from the room—it's
his house, after all,
his house—but he looks at her looking at him and, slowly,
hating her, hating
himself, he moves toward her again, and he's filled suddenly
with frantic passion,
pinning her violently to the mattress, fucking her brains out,
screwing her till she screams.

The Luminous Children

The night after she leaves him for the last time
he finds himself, numb, half-drunk, at the edge
of a lake in cold California mountains: pine scent,
oak smoke. It's placid, unmoving, ready
for winter ice to cover it over. His breath
is white in the darkness. On the water,
suspended, some distance off yet perfectly
clear, is a child: a little pale girl, five or six
years old, looking at him with empty,
expressionless eyes. She's motionless.
Her skin—she wears nothing—is the color
of moonlight. My God, he thinks, isn't she
cold? Because he is. He's very cold.

But then he notices another child, this one
a boy, appear, his skin also reflecting
lunar glow. The two of them shine dully
like Christmas ornaments. Another—another
boy—then another, a girl. Child after child
on the still, dark waters. Seven or eight
of them, maybe more. He's not sure. But
as he stares at them he realizes—ah, God—
they look like him. Like her. Like the two of them
together. Her blue eyes, narrow cheekbones;
his strong nose and chin. Her hair. His hair.

He wants to go to them, hold them,
tell them it's all right, everything will be
all right. But no, damn it, nothing is all right
or ever will be again. The water's cold
and he can't walk on it. His arms reach

to them, he cries out: nothing.
The luminous children begin to fade
then, go dark. They grow dim
and blink out, one by one, until they're gone.
He stands at the shore alone, staring alone
into his lost lake of emptiness.

Bottom

Desperate, each day swallowing
panic–poison slithering through
his veins–he marries again. She's
young, pretty, on her way up
as he lumbers and crashes down,
down. He embarrasses himself
with her, poor pathetic old Jack,
past thirty, career a distant memory,
yet when he studies his mirror image
he can see himself still, as he was,
as if the worm-veined eyes, the
crevice-cracked skin were just
makeup to be cold-creamed away
at the end of the performance. And
when he drinks–divine inspiration!–
it happens, at least for a second
or two, time tears away like an old
shroud, leaves him bright, shining,
new. Then his wife comes in, touches him,
smiles, says soft pity words to him,
and he remembers. He tells her
he loves her, or to fuck off–what
difference? All words are the same word
now, a word endlessly said:
Down. Down. Down. Down.

Bons-Bons

They meet in the powder room of the
Stork Club, sultry New York night,
hot jazz shaking the walls: Greta knows
Dietrich instantly. Femme vs. femme,
bitterest rivals—God, she thinks,
what would *Photoplay* do with this scene?
Dietrich is stuffing bon-bons into her mouth
in between drags on her cigarette.
"Dahling!" she cries, as if Greta were
her bosom friend. "Come, have some
with me!" Nodding encouragingly, Dietrich
lifts the box of ice-cream treats toward Greta.
Smiling, Greta takes one, chews its luscious
coldness quickly, borrows Dietrich's
cig, takes a furtive puff. The two of them
alone for a moment, the writhing world
far away: two high school girls sharing
a guilty pleasure. They grin, giggle, understand
in that moment absolutely everything
about the other. "Do you know," says Dietrich,
"I'm so sick and tired of autograph hounds
coming up to me and saying, 'Aren't you
Greta Garbo?' So do you know what I do?
I say, 'Yes, dahling,' and sign 'Greta Garbo'!"

Greta giggles hysterically. "Do you know what?"
she says. "*I* always sign 'Marlene Dietrich'!"

Past Tense

Another year. Another wife: this one
even milkier in his memory than the last.
When he leaves a room she's in, it's as if
she never existed. But she'll outlive him,
he knows, one day. So will the rest.
All his wives will outlive him, picnic
in the sun when he's dead and the world
doesn't end. So will Greta. And Lillian
Gish. And Clara Bow. And Louis B.
Mayer. And King Vidor. Von Stroheim.
Keaton, Chaplin, Lloyd. The maid—
the one he can still afford to keep.
The cook. He sees it very suddenly,
very certainly. Something lodges within him
this night as he sits with a drink and looks
down at the Hollywood lights on this eve
of this Year of Our Lord 1936. He hears
bells tolling somewhere, in a church maybe,
or in his head. He stares deep into darkness
and feels for a moment weightless,
insubstantial, as if he's already passed
into that other nothingness, is already
past tense, bones and veins folding closed
in the dark, mind skidding into forever.

The Ringing

He remembers calling her once,
or thinks he remembers, long distance
to New York—one night, or perhaps
it was morning. It was her private
number—he thinks he recalls this—
and the operator's breath caught audibly
when he'd said he wanted to put in a call
to Miss Greta Garbo, at this number.
You're John Gilbert, aren't you?
he thinks the woman said to him.
I recognized your voice, she perhaps said.

An interminable wait, he believes
he remembers, many minutes, maybe
hours, until finally a man's words sprang
icily at him: *Miss Garbo is unavailable.*
How did you obtain this number, please?
Bastard! he thinks he thought, perhaps said:
I'm no blasted fan, I'm not to be kicked
off the line and forgotten, I'm more to her
than you can ever imagine, and he
suspects he said this, and perhaps he did.
But the line went dead anyway.

His mind filled then, he thinks it filled
with images of underground, dialing a phone
from within a coffin, suffocating darkness,
the phone ringing, ringing forever,
somewhere else, a place it would never
stop ringing, but it was not a ring at all,
not really, rather a scream, his, many screams,
thousands of them, short, sharp, unheeded,
screaming unnoticed into eternity.
He thinks he remembers this. Remembers
the ringing. Remembers the screaming.

Greta Famous

Oh my Lord Miss Garbo I can't believe it's you I mean really you I'm your biggest fan I saw *Anna Christie* twelve times I cried buckets I have your pictures all over my bedroom wall Miss Garbo you're so beautiful the most beautiful woman in the world no I mean it I really do you've changed my life please yes I know you must board your ship to Sweden I know your sister Alva just died I read it in the paper I'm sorry so sorry Miss Garbo but Miss Garbo could I have an autograph a picture could you come have coffee with me before you go because I think that you could understand me you only you Miss Garbo because I get so lonely sometimes so lonely I just want to die and I look at your pictures and know you could understand me if I could just get you to listen *listen* I love you don't go please stay just one minute one minute Miss Garbo one lousy minute Miss Garbo wait for God's sake wait I don't understand you Miss Garbo is that all I mean to you I'm not a lump of dirt you know Miss Garbo I'm not a piece of shit who the fuck do you think you are all hoity-toity I've spent my life loving you is that all I am to you Miss Garbo you bitch is it is that all I am to you is that all I am

Memories of Greta

His face is on the floor, his cheek pressed coldly
against the bathroom tiles. He beholds her face,
there, floating just above his eyes: realizes no,
it isn't her, not his Greta, not Keta Gustafsson
from the slums of Stockholm (where she said
she'd take him one day, and didn't), but rather
Garbo the movie star, remote, forbidding, breathtaking
but two-dimensional, whites, blacks, grays, untouchable
as light. Where is Greta? he asks himself, reaching
for the bottle which he knows is somewhere
behind him. Where is his Greta, his Keta? He tries
to shake the movie image of her away, but when he does
he finds nothing remains. Were her eyes blue? Was her skin
pale? Her fingers slender? What did she look like?
What did her palm feel like in his? Or her lips?
Gone, gone!...It grows dark in the bathroom where,
once upon a time, she showered, shaved her legs,
made laughing love to him on the floor–she did, here,
here–and Jack struggles still for the bottle, everything
that's vanished sinking, dissolving–white light
melting–memory blinking black in the onrushing night.

Gilbert-Garbo. Garbo-Gilbert. Garbo.

Jack, deep in his cups, cheek resting against the cold
white tile of the master bathroom, has a sudden
moment of clarity: he sees it all. Billing, he thinks,
is the metaphor—the perfect metaphor for...Well,
everything; life itself! In 1915 he'd been
an extra riding horses in Thomas Ince pictures;
no billing at all, no existence, nothing, no one.
Then came *The Apostle of Vengeance,* his name
far down the list, just a baby, and *A Princess*
in the Dark, higher, higher still, growing, and soon
it was *The Merry Widow* and *La Boheme* and
The Big Parade and he was arrived to adulthood,
power, love, a man as large as any man—larger!
In *Flesh and the Devil* and *Love* there was
no question. Then sound, like a disease of age,
sank into his bones—he pictures this, in his mind,
reaching for the whiskey bottle overturned on the
bathroom floor—pictures his bones vibrating
with sound waves, his entire body quivering from within
like a frog on a dissection table, like Frankenstein's
creature jerked into an absurd parody of life.
Sound, sound! Old now at thirty-two, thirty-three,
old as an athlete becomes old, all instantly.
By *Queen Christina* Greta was the star, had been
for years; Jack Gilbert in small print down the list,
someone only partly remembered, like an old
relative in a home. The name dropping, dropping
from print, from memory, until: no more name.
Gone, as he was gone before he was born. Nothing,
not even a ghost. Jack's eyes roll back in his head,
show whites that are blood-red, then gray,
then black. He dies, without a sound.

Home

The room is immense,
more vast than any room should
or could be. He's alone in it
and his cheek is pressed to the tile
floor. But the room grows, inflates,
walls slide back, back again,
the ceiling lifts, the floor stretches
like slick taffy…Or is it, he wonders,
blinking, is it that he himself
is shrinking? Legs, arms, fingers
narrowing, retracting, becoming
smaller, smaller still,
until he's tiny enough at last
to fit. He closes his eyes. Yes,
he's there, in his mother's pocket,
nestled next to her, enveloped,
shielded from the hard world
outside. *Those children have homes,*
he ponders, *and I have a home.*
He feels her palm gently
on him. He's there. He thinks
he's there. He dies, without a sound.

The Waves

Cheek pressed to the tile floor,
he sees a flood rushing at him,
endless waves, blue-boiling, like those
of the Wasatch River that buoyed him
into this life: and he's afraid.
But they pass through him,
slide into the black regions between
his atoms and molecules, become him....

The waves reverse then, recede,
like backwards-running film
in a cheap comedy short, they shrink
and crumple—blossoms in winter—
and he knows in the final moment
that he's going with them, he's
part of them, not separate. He feels
himself rise, tumble, disintegrate.
He dies, without a sound.

News of Jack's Death

She dreams that night
of wasps: their wings hugely
humming, their hard
exoskeletal bodies flying
at her, at her face, her eyes,
and she's in a hot place,
sultry, some place deeply
American, perhaps southern,
a dark city where she doesn't
belong, and she's walking nude
down a sodden street with
people, wasp-faced people
jabbing at her skin, stinging,
biting her, tearing away
bits of her flesh like raw dough,
pale and bloodless, and
the humming turns to static,
to thunder, grows finally
to a sound she recognizes
as applause, painful, deafening
applause crashing down on her
like stones from a vengeful sky.

Garbo Triumphant

Money in hand, enough for ten lifetimes—
she knows, she's counted it—Greta retires,
and dies. No one, not even she, knows
quite when, but she does. Garbo goes on,
eternal celebrity, famous eventually
just for saying *I vant to be alone:*
to Garbo, no matter. She travels, is feted
by royalty, fucks pretty boys. Decades
drift past, unnoticed. Sycophants
stare at her and ask, after she leaves rooms,
that no one sit where she's sat. She laughs
at Truman Capote's gossip in Switzerland,
almost acts again for Tennessee Williams:
The Pink Bedroom. But no. For acting,
Garbo would need Greta: and Greta's dead.
Garbo's finally, perfectly, absolutely Garbo.

Except, sometimes, at night. Adream,
she'll see Jack's eyes inches from her own:
she'll cry out, wake; weep. But only
for a while. Soon enough his eyes
swirl into other eyes, The Director's eyes,
her father's eyes, she'll dream all her life
of eyes. Greta's alive then, in those moments,
with Garbo, in their souls' dark. But a whiskey
or Seconal beats her back again, silences her,
and it's all Garbo once more: Garbo victorious,
Garbo triumphant, Garbo alone at last.

The Lost World

1

New York, 1985. She stares thoughtlessly
out the car window at the pimps and XXX
theaters, hears horns bleat and sirens
wail. All tiresome, so inexpressibly dull.

2

A side street, now: a dilapidated movie
house, one of the original palaces–late 20's
style, Art Deco, all swooping curves
and angles, gray and decrepit now but

3

standing, at least, still standing. There isn't
even a lighted marquee, just a poster
under a buzzing bulb: *The Original*
Silent Classic–Greta Garbo in 'Love'!

4

She sits beside the woman she pays
to attend her, give her her pills and injections
as required. The theater's half-empty.
Tinny dubbed music jerks along to the images

5

that skid up onto the screen: a tired print,
spliced and scratched, jumpy in spots,
in and out of focus–Like herself, she thinks
humorlessly. The girl up there is a stranger,

6

pretty but talentless. And that Vronsky?
A showoff. The worst kind of old-style
cornball movie acting, all sham, ridiculous.
She's angry at herself for insisting on this—

8

why couldn't she have stayed home, watched
television?—she's missing *Dallas*, for God's
sake! What had she wanted here, what had she
wished to find? It's all dead, anyway, gone,

8

lost, all of it. The girl on screen means
nothing to her, nor the man. Not even
ghosts. Ah, God: they gaze into each other's
eyes, Anna and Vronsky, Anna tilts back

9

her head. Someone in the theater
starts to laugh then, a burbling chuckle
that spreads at light speed to others
and soon the whole place is laughing,

10

whooping hysterically at the overblown
inanities on the screen. *Take your top off!*
someone screams at Anna. *Do her, grandpa!*
shouts another, toward Vronsky.

11

She's motionless in her seat, still
as granite. Does she want to leave? asks
her attendant. She doesn't respond,
just stares at the ancient, brittle images,

12

listens to the hooting of the crowd (and
pictures, for an instant, eyes she's not
seen in half a century—men's
eyes, so many men's eyes, Jack's,

13

The Director's, even her father's
in the hard dim room at Blekingegatan 32,
her mind rushing suddenly backward,
tumbling over itself in wild tapestries

14

of remembrance that she crumples
immediately in her brain's fist). The hell
with it, anyway. She's old, very old, and
she hurts, every part of her hurts, hurts

15

all the time, and so she's too old
for such stupid nonsense, too goddamned
old. Beaten. She watches Vronsky lean
toward Anna, watches them kiss

16

as if no one in the world
had ever kissed, the image forty feet
high—no, four hundred, four thousand feet—
and begins to laugh with the rest of them,

17

dry, curdled laughter, derisive, mocking
laughter, such laughter, laughter enough
to wake the dead, if the dead can ever
be wakened, or wish to be.

Afterword

Though based on fact, this "romance in poems" should not be taken as biography. After all, "romance" refers not only to a story of love, but also, according to my *Random House Dictionary of the English Language*, a "narrative depicting heroic or marvelous deeds, pageantry, romantic exploits, etc., usually in a historical or imaginary setting." There was certainly something heroic and marvelous about both John Gilbert and Greta Garbo, and I have allowed myself complete creative freedom in imagining their intimate inner lives. As for the setting, Hollywood often seems both historical *and* imaginary. "When the legend becomes fact," a character in a John Ford film once famously said, "print the legend." It's a dictum I've kept very much in mind while writing *Gilbert and Garbo in Love*.

C.C.

About the Capital Collection

The Capital Collection is an imprint by The Word Works that features excellence in poetry from authors in the Greater Washington, DC area. The hallmark of this series is that each book selected is financially supported by advance book sales and community contributions. The author also agrees to work with the press to promote the Capital Collection books, support other activities of The Word Works, and increase public interest in poetry.

The following individuals have contributed to the Capital Collection to make this book possible

PATRON

Miles David Moore
Hilary Tham

DONOR

Karren L. Alenier
Amruta A. Fernbach
Beau & Linda Kaplan
Elaine Mack
Jane Nelson
Larry Ozanne & Marilyn Metz

About the Author

Photo by Dave Mullen

CHRISTOPHER CONLON'S poems, stories, and articles have appeared in such widely varied publications as *America Magazine, The Washington Post, Poet Lore, Filmfax,* and *Tennessee Williams Annual Review.* His numerous tales for *The Long Story* literary journal are collected in *Saying Secrets: American Stories* (Writers Club Press), and he is the author of a poetry chapbook, *What There Is* (Argonne House Press). A former Peace Corps Volunteer, Conlon now lives in Silver Spring, Maryland. His website can be accessed at www.christopherconlon.com.

About The Word Works

THE WORD WORKS, a nonprofit literary organization, publishes contemporary poetry in collectors' editions. Since 1981, the organization has sponsored the Washington Prize, a $1,500 award to an American poet. Monthly, Word Works presents free literary programs in the Chevy Chase Café Muse series, and each summer, free poetry programs are held at the historic Joaquin Miller Cabin in Washington, DC's Rock Creek Park. Annually, two high school students debut in the Miller Cabin Series as winners of the Young Poets Competition.

Since 1974, WORD WORKS programs have included: "In the Shadow of the Capitol," a symposium and archival project on the African-American intellectual community in segregated Washington, DC; the Gunston Arts Center Poetry Series (Ai, Carolyn Forché, Stanley Kunitz, among others); the Poet-Editor panel discussions at the Bethesda Writer's Center (John Hollander, Maurice English, Anthony Hecht, Josephine Jacobsen, and others); Poet's Jam, a multi-arts program series featuring poetry in performance; a poetry workshop at the Center for Creative Non-Violence (CCNV) shelter. Master Class workshops (Agha Shahid Ali, Thomas Lux, Marilyn Nelson) and the Arts Retreat in Tuscany are ongoing programs.

In 2003, WORD WORKS will have published 51 titles, including work from such authors as Deirdra Baldwin, J.H. Beall, Christopher Bursk, John Pauker, Edward Weismiller, and Mac Wellman. Currently, Word Works publishes occasional anthologies and books under three imprints: the Washington Prize, the Capital Collection and International Editions.

Past grants have been awarded by the National Endowment for the Arts, National Endowment for the Humanities, DC Commission on the Arts & Humanities, Witter Bynner Foundation, Writer's Center, Bell Atlantic, Batir Foundation, and others, including many generous private patrons.

THE WORD WORKS has established an archive of artistic and administrative materials in the Washington Writing Archive housed in the George Washington University Gelman Library.

Please enclose a self-addressed, stamped envelope with all inquiries.

Word Works Books

Karren L. Alenier, *Wandering on the Outside*
Karren L. Alenier, ed., *Whose Woods These Are*
Karren L. Alenier, Hilary Tham, Miles David Moore, eds.,
Winners: A Retrospective of the Washington Prize
* Nathalie F. Anderson, *Following Fred Astaire*
* Michael Atkinson, *One Hundred Children Waiting for a Train*
Mel Belin, *Flesh That Was Chrysalis* (CAPITAL COLLECTION)
* Peter Blair, *Last Heat*
Doris Brody, *Judging the Distance* (CAPITAL COLLECTION)
Christopher Bursk, ed., *Cool Fire*
Grace Cavalieri, *Pinecrest Rest Haven* (CAPITAL COLLECTION)
Moshe Dor, Barbara Goldberg, Giora Leshem, eds.,
The Stones Remember
Isaac Goldberg, *Solomon Ibn Gabirol: A Bibliography of His Poems in Translation* (INTERNATIONAL EDITIONS)
* Linda Lee Harper, *Toward Desire*
James Hopkins, *Eight Pale Women*
* Ann Rae Jonas, *A Diamond Is Hard But Not Tough*
Myong-Hee Kim, *Crow's Eye View: The Infamy of Lee Sang, Korean Poet* (INTERNATIONAL EDITIONS)
Vladimir Levchev, *Black Book of the Endangered Species* (INTERNATIONAL EDITIONS)
* Fred Marchant, *Tipping Point*
Miles David Moore, *The Bears of Paris* (CAPITAL COLLECTION)
Jacklyn Potter, Dwaine Rieves, Gary Stein, eds.
Cabin Fever: Poets at Joaquin Miller's Cabin
* Jay Rogoff, *The Cutoff*
Robert Sargent, *Aspects of a Southern Story*
Robert Sargent, *A Woman From Memphis*
* Enid Shomer, *Stalking the Florida Panther*
Maria Terrone, *The Bodies We Were Loaned* (CAPITAL COLLECTION)
Hilary Tham, *Bad Names for Women* (CAPITAL COLLECTION)
Hilary Tham, *Counting* (CAPITAL COLLECTION)
* Miles Waggener, *Phoenix Suites*
* Charlotte Gould Warren, *Gandhi's Lap*
* George Young, *Spinoza's Mouse*

* *Washington Prize winners*